Marbles

Cathy Hope

CELEBRATION PRESS
Pearson Learning Group

Safety Tips

- Glass containers are too dangerous to carry marbles in. A cloth drawstring bag is safer.
- Be careful not to leave marbles around after you have finished playing.

  —Marbles are dangerous if young children or babies put them in their mouths.

  —People can slip on marbles left on the floor.

Words for Marbles in Other Languages

Danish	*kugler*
Dutch	*knikkeren*
French	*billes*
German	*Murmeln*
Greek	*gazés* (glass marbles), *vólous* (clay marbles)
Indonesian	*guli*
Italian	*il gioco delle birille*
Japanese	*ohajiki*
Latvian	*murmuli*
Maltese	*boċċe*
Mandarin	*da dan zi*
Spanish	*canicas*
Turkish	*bilye mishet*
Vietnamese	*choi bi*

Contents

Marbles Crazes

One of the world's oldest known games is marbles. Marbles is a long time favorite of children in many countries. Admiring, collecting, counting, swapping, and bargaining are just as much fun as playing the game. Many adults play marbles too!

Playing marble games can be catching. A marbles craze can happen at any time or any place and last for several weeks or months, then suddenly disappear.

MARBLE NAMES

Marble names can vary from school to school, place to place, or country to country.

- Hot Lips
- Cat's Eye
- Red Back

- Spaghetti
- Snake
- Warm
- Ropey

- Petrol
- Oily
- Mirror
- Cokey

- Stardust
- Galaxy
- Disco
- City

- Egg
- Honeysuckle
- Banana
- Yolky

- Tomato
- Red Pearl
- Lipstick
- Volcano

When you swap your marbles, work out a fair exchange. You might decide
- One Spaghetti marble is worth five Cat's Eyes
- One Galaxy marble is worth two Tomatoes

Marbles Through the Ages

3000 B.C.
Stone and pottery marbles belonging to a child who lived more than 5,000 years ago, were found in an Egyptian grave.

1700s
It is thought that the name **marbles** originated more than 300 years ago when they were made from a stone called marble.

Blue and brown glazed pottery marbles used in kettles in the 1800s

Late 1800s
From the 1870s, most hand made glass marbles were produced in Germany. Some were also made in Venice, Italy. These glass marbles were very rare and highly valued.

| 3000 B.C. | 27 B.C. | B.C. | A.D. | 1700 | 1800 |

27 B.C.
Marbles from Roman times more than 2,000 years ago were found in the Thames River in England. Even the Roman Emperor Augustus liked playing marbles in his spare time.

1800s
Porcelain and pottery marbles were made from clay and fired in kilns. Marbles made this way in China were often hand painted. Small pottery balls were used in iron kettles to prevent rusting. Children often used these to play marbles.

1890s
During the 1890s, machines were first used to make glass marbles. Children collected clear glass stoppers from the tops of lemonade bottles to use as marbles.

Agate marbles

Marbles tournament

1900s

A factory in Germany produced many wonderful marbles from agate and other semiprecious stones. These marbles are very hard and durable and are excellent shooters.

1949

"Cat's Eyes" marbles began to be manufactured in the United States. Today they are still made in Paden City, West Virginia.

1900　　　　**1920**　　　　**1940**　**1949**　→

1920s

The National Marbles Tournament began at Wildwood, New Jersey in 1923. In Great Britain the game of marbles became a competitive sport in 1926. Tournaments are held every year.

1939–1945

Children found it difficult to buy marbles during World War II.

Hand made marbles

Learn How to Flick Marbles

Once you master the skill of flicking a marble, you will soon be able to shoot the marble with accuracy. The marble you select to fire is called the "shooter" or "taw".

There are two effective ways to flick a marble.

Ordinary Flick

This is a one-handed flick.

1. Select the hand you wish to shoot with. Make sure at least one or more of your knuckles rests on the ground. This is called "to knuckle down" or "knuckling".

2. Bend your thumb at the first joint, and tuck it under your curled index finger. Balance the shooter marble in front of your thumbnail and hold it securely.

3. Look at the target marble you wish to hit.

4. Release your thumb quickly, flicking the shooter marble and propelling it forward.

Double Flick

You'll need both hands for this method and with practice, this is a fast and accurate flick.

1 With your right hand resting on the ground, hold the shooter marble between your thumb and pointer finger.

2 With your left hand, make an arch with your thumb and pointer finger.

3 The middle finger of the left hand acts like a trigger and needs to be held back as far as possible by the middle finger of the right hand.

4 Look at your target marble, and release the middle finger of your left hand against the shooter marble.

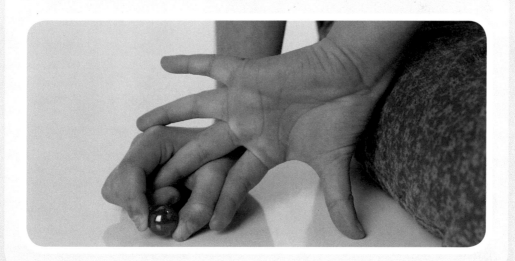

Rules for Marbles Games

Rules can vary from place to place, game to game, and player to player. Decide on the rules before you start playing to stop unnecessary arguments!

SOME IDEAS FOR RULES

Play "for Fair"

When playing with someone younger than you, always play "for fair". Marbles are given back to the owners at the end of the game. Younger players will look up to you if you are fair and happy to share your expertise.

Play "for Keeps"

If another player's marble is hit, the shooter wins it when playing "for keeps". Only play with marbles you are prepared to lose.

Foots or No Foots

Decide what to do if another player's marble hits your foot. If "foots", throw the marble against your shoe so it rebounds.

Drops or No Drops

Decide whether a player may or may not pick up a marble and drop it onto or throw it with force at the marble to be hit. Make sure everyone agrees on the type of marble to be used as the "drop".

Clearance or No Clearance

Decide whether players are allowed to clear away lumps of dirt, sticks, stones, or other obstructions.

Tips or No Tips

"Tips" is when a marble is barely touched by the shooter marble, rather than being hit squarely. "No tips" means a player can't win the marble this way.

Marbles Games

RINGER or BIG RING

Number of Players

2 to 6 players

How to Play

1 With chalk, mark out a circle outdoors about 10 feet in diameter.

2 Mark the center of the circle with an *X*.
Each arm of the *X* should measure about 9 inches.

3 Select 13 marbles to place in the circle.
Place one marble at the center of the *X*.

4 Each player selects a shooter marble and stands outside the circle.

5 Take turns shooting at the marbles in the circle from the chalk line, aiming to knock them out of the circle.

The winner is the person who shoots the most marbles from the circle.

Marbles in position for playing Ringer.

BOUNCE EYE

Number of Players

2 or more players

Tom Bowlers are giant marbles and Semi-Toms are mid-sized marbles.

How to Play

1 Play this game on bare ground. Mark out a small ring with a stick.

2 Each player places a marble in the center of the ring.

3 Each player selects a marble to use to drop into the ring. Tom Bowlers and Semi-Toms are ideal.

4 Decide if the game is for "for keeps" or "for fair".

5 Hold your marble at eye level and drop it into the pool of marbles, aiming to knock a marble out of the ring. Retrieve the marble you dropped into the ring.

When you are playing "for keeps", you win any marbles you have knocked outside the ring.

Making the ring for Bounce Eye

Players hold their marble at eye level before dropping it into the pool of marbles.

TRACKS or ROLLY DOWN the GUTTER

Number of Players

2 or more players

How to Play

1 Decide on a track, pathway, or gutter for the game, or mark out a winding track in sand or dirt.

2 Select one marble each to play with.

3 The first player stands at the start of the track and flicks a marble along the track. The next player then flicks a marble to follow.

4 If a player's marble is hit, that player must start again.

The winner is the first person to reach the end of the track.

The winner is the first person to reach the end of the track.

WALLS or REBOUNDS

Number of Players

As many as you wish

How to Play

1 Select several marbles that others might like to win, and you are prepared to lose.

2 Find a wall to shoot marbles against so they rebound or bounce back.

3 Each player chooses some marbles to place near the wall.

4 Each player takes turns to shoot a marble at the wall. If you hit a marble as your marble rebounds, you keep it.

If your shooter marble doesn't hit a marble when it rebounds, it becomes one of the target marbles.

Each player takes a turn to shoot a marble at the wall.

How Marbles Are Made

You can buy a spectacular range of colored and patterned marbles.

China, Taiwan, and Mexico are the main producers of marbles. West Virginia, in the United States, has a history of marble manufacturing, and marbles are still made there.

1

Unwanted colored glass bottles, bowls, glasses, and pieces of broken glass are recycled to make marbles. The glass is broken into small pieces, then melted down in huge glass furnaces.

2

Blobs of red-hot molten glass are squeezed out of a nozzle and dropped onto turning rollers that shape the marbles.

3

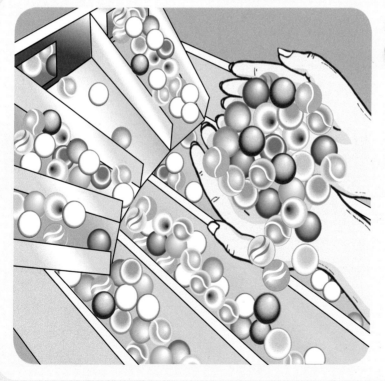

After cooling, the marbles are inspected before packaging.

Make Your Own Marbles

Sunbaked Clay or Kiln-Fired Pottery Marbles

Try making marbles from real clay. After rolling your marbles, bake them in the sun. When rock hard, paint and varnish them. If you have a pottery kiln at school, you may be able to have your clay marbles fired, then glazed.

Air-Drying Modeling Clay Marbles

You Will Need

✔ air-drying modeling clay from craft stores (in a variety of colors)

✔ paper towel

✔ fine sandpaper

✔ water-based paints (if using white clay)

✔ clear varnish

METHOD

1 Dampen your hands slightly.

2 Take only enough clay for one marble at a time, and close the container until you need more. You can combine colors.

3 Knead the clay, then roll it into a round ball the size of a marble.

4 Dry your marbles on a paper towel for at least 24 hours.

5 When dry, sand the marbles so they are smooth.

6 If using white clay, paint your marbles using any designs you wish.

7 Varnish the marbles and let them dry before using them.

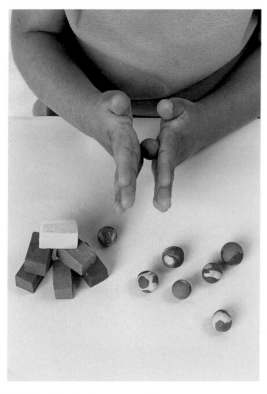

Roll the clay to form a marble.

Sand the marbles so they are smooth.

Index